I0164179

Schooling

The

Nations

... dominion driven by love.

By Rev. James DuJack

Schooling The Nations

Copyright © 2012 by Rev. James DuJack

All rights reserved. This book or any portion thereof
may not be reproduced or used in any manner
whatsoever without the express written permission
of the publisher except for the use of brief
quotations in a book review.

Printed in the United States of America

First Printing, 2012

ISBN-13: 978-0615718989
ISBN-10: 0615718981

Oakwood Covenant Press
260 Oakwood Avenue
Troy, NY 12182

Scripture Quotations are from The Holy Bible,

King James Version

DEDICATION:
To Patrick Martin, my best man, who
schooled me in Christ, and on the hard court.

Schooling The Nations is the re-working of a
sermon given in September, 2012 to the
Saints at Oakwood Bible Church

Contents

GOD'S UNIVERSITY:

THE SCHOOL OF LAW

THE SCHOOL OF HISTORY

THE SCHOOL OF PHILOSOPHY

THE SCHOOL OF PROPHECY

THE SCHOOL OF LOVE

Chapter 1:
INTRODUCING GOD'S UNIVERSITY

Isaiah 41:1,8, 28 & 29 "Keep silence before me, O islands; and let the people renew their strength: let them come near; then let them speak; let us come near unto judgment. For I beheld, and there was no man; even among them, and there was no counselor, that, when I asked of them, could answer a word. Behold, they are all vanity; their works are nothing: their molten images are wind and confusion".

"Schooling The Nations": School is back in session. Many harbor the sentiment, some are willing to say it; there even exists a subset who are willing to celebrate and sing, "it's the most wonderful time of the year". Next Tuesday marks back to school night here at OCS. Also on Tuesday, I'll be back to school at the Alliance Theological Seminary for orientation. Having taken a thirty year break from my Graduate studies, for me it will be "Back to School".

Schooling is about learning a particular subject matter. Here in Isaiah 41 God is going to teach the nations. But there is another kind of schooling; the street-slang definition, the playground definition. Schooling someone, taking them to school; is about showing them how it's really done, whipping them in a contest. There is a not so hidden humiliation in this type of schooling.

9

About two weeks ago, for me the first time, I was drawn into a FIFA, (XBOX thumbs game), soccer contest against Andrew. He graciously adjusted the program to its most basic, elemental level; still Andrew schooled me!

The Schooling of The Nations found here in Isaiah 41 is of both kinds.

- There is the legitimate teaching of a lesson. There is the desire and invitation into formal and fraternal learning.

- But as often happens with the rebellious, proud, and arrogant subjects, **there is a schooling.**

The nations, their wise men, their idols are schooled. They are humiliated, defeated, they are reduced to silence. They begin, being charged to enter God's classroom in an orderly, respectful silence.

Isaiah 41:1 "Keep silence before me, O islands; and let the people renew their strength: let them come near; then let them speak: let us come near together to judgment".

If I could use a popular idiom to describe this, this is what they were doing! YAKING! This is what God wanted them to do: hold their speech, while they began in that orderly, respectful silence. After being schooled, and **schooled,** they are speechless.

Isaiah 41:28,29 "For I beheld, and there was no man; even among them, and there was no counselor, that, when I asked of them, could answer a word. Behold they are all vanity, their works are nothing; their molten images are wind and confusion".

They have nothing to say, they are reduced to silence. After all, they are, as St. Paul noted in First Corinthians 12:2 of the New Testament, "Dumb Idols". The word here is not ignorant, though they were that too! The Greek word is "Aphonos". A negative phonos – sound; (phonograph, telephone, cellphone). They make no sound, they don't speak, they have nothing to say.

God is here **"Schooling The Nations"**. *Isaiah 41:1 "Keep silence before me, O islands; and let the people renew their strength: let them come near; then let them speak: let us come near together to judgment".*

Back to verse 1, these islands, are all the people of the world! They, the Jews, were the land. The "sea" was the gentile world. Therefore, everything associated with the sea; the coastlands, the islands, etc.; were the nations, the gentiles, the heathens.

One of the remarkable aspects of this schooling is that it concerns the historical context. Here it "appears" that the pagans are winning and the people of God are hopelessly languishing in exile, in Babylon.

Now, before we go any further, it is important for us to note that this schooling does not take place in a vacuum or in private. Watching, listening in, auditing this class (if you will) are the Israelites. So much so, that a large portion of this schooling involves a running commentary by God to His Son and Servant, Israel.

Let's look at *Isaiah 41:8*. *"But thou, Israel, art my servant, Jacob whom I have chosen, the seed of Abraham my friend."*

From verse 8 through verses twenty, Israel receives this side lecture; one of great grace and blessing. God is the instructor, and both Israel and the Nations are in on all that He says to each party!!

What a blessing it is to be in on the class, when as a child, your parent is taking someone to school! Proverbs 17:6 says in part, that the glory of children are their fathers.

In the fall of 1946, sixty six years ago, my father, a junior, was a fullback and place kicker for the Catholic High Football Team and was their leading scorer. Though, I obviously was not around then, I could tell you of his exploits on the Gridiron. What I was around for, and far more significant were his exploits on the field of life.

Nonetheless, the Gridiron was a sign of things to come. For the first thirty years of my life, I was able to observe and audit first hand, up close and personal, not his work on a playground or ball field but his tireless self-sacrificing provision for our family, our business, and our community. I, as a son, was able to watch a master at work.

Here in Isaiah 41, Israel gets to do the same and now, it is ours to watch **God School The Nations.** In keeping with our educational theme; and as this is God's Universe, he has a university.

In God's University, we find (among other things):

A school of Law
A school of History
A school of Philosophy
A school of Prophesy
A school of Love

Chapter 2:
THE SCHOOL OF LAW

Looking at verse one; we begin with The School of Law.

Isaiah 41:1 "Keep silence before me, O islands; and let the people renew their strength: let them come near; then let them speak: let us come near together to judgment".

This schooling is judicial, (judgment). "Come near, approach the bar." There is order, there are legal procedures, and there is etiquette in view here. God is going to lay out His case. The pagans, their wise men, their idols, they are also to be afforded a case for their arguments. Their time, their chance will come. Then let them speak, their formal invitation comes in verse 21.

Isaiah 41:21 "Produce your cause, saith the LORD; bring forth your strong reasons, saith the King of Jacob."

16

Chapter 3:
SCHOOL OF HISTORY

Following this judicial review, God brings them to the **School of History.** Beginning in verse 2, our curriculum brings us to God's work in world history. Verses 2 – 4 come in the form of a question, with God answering, that indeed He is the one who has orchestrated history. What a good teacher God is asking questions. Is this all about His calling of Abraham? Is this also all about His calling of Cyrus? Each were Chaldeans or of the East. Each were servants and friends of God, who led, even delivered God's people. Abraham fathering their birth as a nation and Cyrus fathering their rebirth. The Nations, even the Babylonians are here **schooled in history.**

Chapter 4:
THE SCHOOL OF PHILOSOPHY

Quickly, next they are **schooled in philosophy.** Don't miss the judicial connection to reason, look at verse 1;

Isaiah 41:1 "Keep silence before me, O islands; and let the people renew their strength: let them come near; then let them speak: let us come near together to judgment". Compare this to *Isaiah 1:18 "Come now, and let us reason together, saith the LORD: though your sins be as scarlet, they shall be as white as snow; though they be red like crimson, they shall be as wool."*

God wants to engage them cognitively. He's not, nor has He ever been interested in mindless robots. **Thou shalt love the Lord thy God with all thy heart, soul, mind, and strength.**

Ours is, as Bavinck writes a "Reasonable Faith". Look at *Isaiah 41:21 "Produce your cause, saith the LORD; bring forth your strong reasons, saith the King of Jacob."*

Make your case, bring proofs, provide arguments, establish your reasons. God is very much interested in epistemology: that branch of philosophy regarding "knowledge". People need to "know" things.

*Isaiah 41:22, 23, 26 "Let them bring them forth, and show us what shall happen; let them show the former things, what they be, that we may consider them, and **know** the latter end of them; or declare us things for to come. Show the things that are to come hereafter, that we may **know** that ye are gods; yea, do good, or do evil, that we may be dismayed, and behold it together. Who hath declared from the beginning, that we may **know**; and before time, that we may say, He is righteous? Yea, there is none that showeth, yea, there is none that declareth, yea, there is none that heareth your words."*

God is schooling them in philosophy because He is the one, the only one whereby we may **know** things concerning the future with certainty.

Chapter 5:
SCHOOL OF PROPHECY

This brings us to His school of prophecy. Some of these same verses, but the reference to knowing is all about the prophetic future.

*Isaiah 41:22 – 25, "Let them bring them forth, and show us **what shall happen**; let them show the former things, what they be, that we may consider them, and know **the latter end** of them; or **declare us things for to come**. Show the things that are to come hereafter, that we may know that ye are gods; yea, do good, or do evil, that we may be dismayed, and behold it together. Behold, ye are of nothing, and your work of nought; an abomination is he that chooseth you. I raised up one from the north, and he shall come: from the rising of the sun shall he call upon my name; and he shall come upon princes as upon mortar, and as the potter treadeth clay."*

Here pagan wise men and idols are shamed, schooled and silenced (verse 24). More prophecy is found in verse 25.

Cyrus, (still ahead) is the one who would release Israel from captivity some seventy years later.

This is detailed in *Isaiah 41:27*; *"The first shall say to Zion, behold, behold them: and I will give to Jerusalem one that bringeth good tidings."* It was spoken as prophetic history in *Isaiah 44:28; "That saith of Cyrus, He is my shepherd, and shall perform all my pleasure: even saying to Jerusalem, thou shalt be built; and to the temple, thy foundation shall be laid."*

All this schooling in law, history, philosophy, and prophecy is part of what God is doing in Isaiah 41. But as I mentioned, God's son is listening in and God makes many side bar comments to His son, with the nations listening in.

Chapter 6:
SCHOOL OF LOVE

All this bring us to the School of Love. Allow me to read of this precious schooling in its entirety.

Isaiah 41:8-20 "But thou, Israel, art my servant, Jacob whom I have chosen, the seed of Abraham my friend. Thou whom I have taken from the ends of the earth and called thee from the chief men thereof, and said unto thee, Thou art my servant; I have chosen thee, and not cast thee away. Fear thou not; for I am with thee: be not dismayed; for I am thy God: I will strengthen thee; yea, I will help thee; yea, I will uphold thee with the right hand of my righteousness. Behold, all they that are incensed against thee shall be ashamed and confounded; they shall be as nothing; and they that strive with thee shall perish. Thou shalt seek them, and shalt not find them, even them that contended with thee: they that war against thee shall be as nothing, and as a thing of nought. For I the LORD thy God will hold thy right hand, saying unto thee, Fear not; I will help thee. Fear not, thou worm Jacob, and ye men of Israel I will help thee, saith the LORD and thy redeemer, the Holy One of Israel. Behold, I will make thee a new sharp threshing instrument having teeth: thou shalt thresh the mountains, and beat them small, and shalt make the hills as chaff. Thou shalt fan them, and the wind shall carry them away, and the whirlwind shall scatter them: and thou shalt rejoice in the LORD, and shalt glory in the Holy One of Israel. When the poor and needy seek water, and there is none, and their tongue faileth for thirst, I the LORD will hear them, I the God of Israel will not forsake them. I will open rivers in high places, and fountains in the midst of the valleys: I will make the wilderness a pool of water, and the dry land springs of water. I will plant in the wilderness the cedar, the shittah tree, and the myrtle, and the oil tree; I will set in the desert the fir tree, and the pine, and the box tree together. That they may see, and know, and consider, and understand together, that the hand of the LORD hath done this, and the Holy One of Israel hath created it."

Don't miss (verse 20), that last verse. All this schooling is done in front of all! What a great thing for Israel to hear! What a great thing for the nations to hear! What a great thing for **us** to hear! Precious truths, wonderful comforts, and promises. But did you know, do you know, that these are ours!! That they belong to us!! All this comfort, all this love is ours! This was presented at a time when they were feeling the lowest of the low.

Look at *Isaiah 41:8 "And thou, Israel, art my servant, Jacob whom I have chosen the seed of Abraham my friend."*

Not only are we, the new Israel, His new servants, the new Jacob, the new elect (chosen); but we are His **friends**.

John 15:15 "Henceforth I call you not servants; for the servant knoweth not what his lord doeth; but I have called you friends; for all things that I have heard of my Father I have made known unto you."

Not only are we all those things: we fulfill Isaiah 41:8 wherein is referenced the **seed of Abraham**. Make note of that and then let's look at *Galatians 3:16; "Now to Abraham and his seed were the promises made. He saith not, and to seeds, as of many; but as of one, and to thy seed, which is Christ."* Be sure to connect vs. 26-29 (as 2 Corinthians 1:25 says), all these promises of God **are ours**. They are yea and Amen in Christ Jesus!

All this schooling taking place: the school of law, history, philosophy, prophecy and this wonderful school of love is ours and is **about us**! Soak all those verses in! They are not about nationality, not about birth, but **all** about being born again. What a schoolmaster we have; schooling the nations and bringing us to Christ!

In all this schooling and more, we see God's dominion. A dominion driven by love!

www.ingramcontent.com/pod-product-compliance
Lightning Source LLC
Chambersburg PA
CBHW060608030426
42337CB00019B/3669